VIDEO MODELING

Visual-Based Strategies to Help People on the Autism Spectrum

Stephen Lockwood, BCBA

VIDEO MODELING
Visual-Based Strategies to Help People on the Autism Spectrum

All marketing and publishing rights guaranteed to and reserved by:

FUTURE HORIZONS INC.

721 W. Abram Street
Arlington, TX 76013
(800) 489-0727
(817) 277-0727
(817) 277-2270 (fax)
E-mail: info@fhautism.com
www.fhautism.com

Cover & interior design by John Yacio III

ISBN: 9781941765586

CONTENTS

Introduction...v

1. Peer Mediated Instruction 1

2. Visual Support 3

3. Picture Exchange Communication System 5

4. Pivotal Response Training 7

5. Computer Assisted Instruction 9

6. Getting Started.. 11

    Lights, Camera, Action! 18

7. Building Independence 21

8. Transitions... 25

    Lights, Camera, Action! 32

9. Play Skills.. 35

    Lights, Camera, Action! 37

10. Social Skills.. 39

    Lights, Camera, Action! 42

11. Teaching Skills... 45

    Lights, Camera, Action! 49

12. Vocational Skills... 51

    Lights, Camera, Action! 55

13. Final Scene!.. 57

References... 61

About the Author.. 63

Introduction

There are many evidence-based strategies which have been demonstrated to be effective for individuals with Autism Spectrum Disorder (ASD), such as prompting, reinforcement, task analysis, discrete trial teaching, social skills instruction, extinction, and more. When it comes specifically to technology and modeling, the following are strategies that I have found to be particularly effective based on the learning and behavioral profiles of the individual with ASD.

1. Peer Mediated Instruction

Peer-mediated instruction is a strategy where peers of the target students are trained to provide the necessary tutoring in educational, behavioral, or social concerns (Chan et al. 2009). These peers are then able to mediate appropriate behavior by modeling it themselves, as well as prompting and reinforcing appropriate behavior when it occurs from the target student.

While I was teaching in a middle school, I worked with a general education colleague to construct a "Helping Hands" program. We assembled a group of neurotypical peers that volunteered to be "buddies" with our students. These peers participated in structured group discussions about the needs of our students and how they could best help them. Early activities included structured games in the gymnasium and art projects in our classroom as students began meeting and spending time with their buddies on a weekly basis. Later, our students began getting involved in after-school activities with their buddies, and the culminating activities included trips out into the community together.

2. Visual Support

Visual support refers to the use of pictures (which may be actual photographs or pictures taken from magazines or the internet) as a cue to help a learner perform a skill more independently. This may come in the form of a visual schedule that shows a sequence of activities or the steps to an activity. Many learners with autism respond very positively to visual cues, which can help to make an otherwise abstract concept significantly more concrete.

3. Picture Exchange Communication System

The Picture Exchange Communication System (PECS) is an augmentative communication that is designed to help nonverbal individuals communicate both functionally and effectively. It has also been shown to be effective in verbal students or in preschool settings. While the name may imply that it is only picture cards, a key component to using PECS effectively is that

it is a communication system that goes beyond simply using picture cards to stimulate communication. A child is taught to exchange a picture of an item with a listener who will honor the request for the item in the picture. This is later expanded to convey requests or to express needs or emotions. PECS is

child-initiated and is both easily understood and implemented, and can be individually tailored to be functional to the needs of a specific person. The portability of the system gives it a universal appeal (Ball 2008). PECS is also utilized in the software of augmentative devices, where the pictures can be touched and the device will speak the desired words.

4. Pivotal Response Training

Pivotal Response Training (PRT) is an Applied Behavior Analysis (ABA)-based behavioral intervention that suggests two behaviors are "pivotal" to the acquisition of other behaviors, those two behaviors being motivation (reinforcement) and the ability to respond to multiple cues. Children are taught in naturalistic settings and components include child-choice, turn-taking, and the reinforcement of all attempts. It is used to target language skills, play skills, and social behavior, and is child-directed and uses reinforcement directly related to the task (Ball 2008).

5. Computer Assisted Instruction

Computer-assisted instruction refers to situations in which an instruction is presented through a computer to a student, or the computer itself is a platform for an interactive learning environment. It uses a combination of text, graphics, sound, and video to enhance and facilitate the learning process, and it can be used to personalize instruction for learners with lan-

guage limitations, physical limitations, or learning disabilities. For example, a screen-reading program may assist a learner whose sight is impaired, or an oversized keyboard may assist a learner with limited fine motor control.

However, the most effective strategy that I have encountered during my career is the utilization of video modeling. Video modeling is an instructional teaching technique that utilizes assistive technology and videos as the primary vehicle. It is a strategy that has applications regardless of ability or age. It has a growing research base and can be used to teach a variety of skills, including social skills, play skills, and more.

Video modeling typically has three core components:

1. Video recording the individual to be taught or someone else, or finding commercially made videos highlighting the behavior to be taught.

2. The video is used to teach the skills.

3. The individual is required to perform the skill.

Video modeling is by no means a new idea. Even in the 1980s, it was identified as a time-efficient and personnel-conserving teaching tool (Charlop and Milstein 1989). However, the technology available today makes this technique invaluable and essential in teaching going forward.

In this book, we will be discussing the process of developing, implementing, and assessing video modeling for learners with autism to increase independence, facilitate learning, and improve quality of life.

6. Getting Started

Technology has come a long way from the days of video cassette players, when it may have been cumbersome to record a video and a necessity to have a television available to play it back. Nowadays, it is possible to record an impromptu video in a matter of seconds with a cell phone, and with these advances in technology comes new avenues and opportunities for teaching and training using video technology. With the immediacy and ease of video capture technology, there has never been a better time to incorporate video modeling throughout programming.

There is a plethora of resources available now to create a video for the purposes of video modeling, ranging from traditional hand-held camera,

to a webcam, to a cell phone camera. While the portability and ease-of-access of a cell phone can make it convenient to create a quick video for immediate use, there are times when the crisper presentation of a traditionally filmed video will be more appropriate. The context of the situation will dictate what is best to use.

Similarly, it is important to consider the perspective that will be

11

most beneficial for a video to take. While sometimes we will want to use a video from a third-person perspective (in which the viewer is watching a person complete the targeted behavior), there are situations where it will be most beneficial to show a first-person perspective—or a "mind's eye" perspective—in which the viewer is seeing precisely what they will be seeing out of their own eyes when they perform the desired behavior.

While working with students to increase their independence in job skills, we created a series of videos showing vocational tasks—such as simple assembly work with nuts and bolts or wrapping hamburgers—being completed from the first-person "mind's eye" perspective. While watching the video, they saw a first-person perspective of my hands as I completed the task. However, we ran into the problem that some tasks required measuring  with a ruler or cup, or filing according to a letter, and on the video it was difficult if not impossible to see these small details. This made it difficult to follow exactly what was being expected and performed. Our solution was to take still pictures or close-up video of the ruler being used, or the tab being filed, and splice this into the video at the appropriate time to look at it. It was then possible to fully follow and imitate the task being performed.

There is a misconception that a key component of this is that the learner needs to have the pre-requisite skills necessary to access and view a video, such as attending to the video or access skills (turning the device on, or swiping or otherwise manipulating a touch screen to access and view the video). This does not always prove to be true in practice. Even students who do not have a history of engagement in videos have been successful when video modeling is implemented in an appropriate manner. The true key components to having success with video modeling are repetition, exposure, and predictability, all of which can lead over time to successful engagement and positive behavior. The video should be accessible in a regular and predictable way.

Before creating a video, select a behavior to target. It is vital that the targeted behavior be measurable and observable. For example, the targeted behavior should not be "Danny will improve his social skills" or "Jamie will dress correctly." More appropriate goals may be "Danny will initiate

appropriate social interaction by saying 'hello' to a peer when he joins morning group" or "Jamie will put on pants independently."

Collect baseline data on the skill before beginning the video process, as this information can inform the type of video that is created. As when teaching any skill, it is important to know what the learner is already able to do, particularly identifying specific steps that can already be completed without assistance. A video may not be necessary for steps that are already known, but may be needed to contextualize later steps depending on the skill.

When it comes time to actually create our video, determine who will be an appropriate person to use as a model. Ultimately, the video needs to display a person performing the targeted skill both appropriately and independently. If the learner will want to watch him or herself, record a video of them being prompted through the task, and then edit the video to remove the prompts. Would the learner prefer to watch a parent, teacher, sibling, or peer? If the learner will not show increased interest from watching a familiar person, it may be possible to save time by searching the web to see if a video model for this skill already exists.

Consider how best to prepare the environment in which the video will be viewed. Where and when should the video be watched? How many times, or how long should it be viewed for? Ideally, the skill should be performed in a natural setting in which it would normally occur, with the skill be used in a functional way. For example, a personal care skill such as brushing teeth would be performed in a bathroom, or a food preparation skill performed in a kitchen. Any materials being used should match the materials that appear in the video.

When it comes time to view the video, keep in mind the pre-requisite skill of being able to attend to a video for several minutes without exhibiting challenging behavior (Delano 2007). Even with this skill in place, prompts may be necessary to maintain attention to the video. Whenever possible, do not prompt performance of the actual skill, but rather prompt or redirect attention to the video. Allow the learner the opportunity to watch the video multiple times before attempting the skill. In some cases, particularly longer chain tasks, it will be appropriate to stop or repeat the video after individual steps. In other cases, viewing the whole video will work best—just as in task-analysis, when we consider whether to teach a skill total-task or in steps.

Additionally, it is important that the idea of watching the video is not presented as "work." Just let it play until it becomes second-nature in the environment, and the learner gets used to it and begins to gravitate towards it on his or her own. Put the video on a loop and let it run until the learner engages with it. For those learners that seem to not be interested in videos, again, just give them exposure until they begin to be interested.

While monitoring the program in progress, it is vital to collect data on both the performance of the skill as well as the viewing of the video so that informed and data-driven decisions can be made. Take note of the trend of the data being collected. While the learner may not necessarily have mastered the skill, they may be making smaller strides towards it. As long as data is trending towards success, alterations may not be necessary. However, if after three to five sessions progress is not being made or trending downward, it is time to troubleshoot.

At this point, it is best to assume nothing and consider each of the following:

- Is the video being used frequently enough?
- Is the video being utilized properly (whole-viewing versus partial viewing)?
- Is the learner attending to the video, or able to attend to the video?
- Has staff received sufficient training on how to properly utilize the video?
- Are appropriate and sufficient prompting strategies being utilized?
- Is sufficient and appropriate reinforcement being provided?
- Is the video appropriate for the learner or is to too complex?

Once success is achieved and progress has been made, begin the fading process. A video being viewed on a computer screen can be faded to a cell phone or a tablet. We may fade the length of a video, showing it fewer times or perhaps only showing the first few steps of a task to get the learner started, and shortening the length of time viewed or the number of steps shown.

It may not always be an appropriate goal to fade out a video entirely. Daily planners are, in essence, a visual schedule that many people utilize in everyday life with no intention of ceasing usage, nor would anyone think that they should. I readily admit to the fact that I have made it into my thirties and have no idea how to tie a tie. If the fate of humanity rested on my ability to conjure up a Windsor knot on the fly, humanity would be doomed. However, on an as-needed basis, I can use my computer or phone to access a video on how to tie a tie, and follow the model. Given the infrequent basis of which I actually need a tie around my neck, this works just fine.

Lights, Camera, Action!

Johnny's parents would like him to learn how to brush his teeth appropriately. A baseline assessment shows that while he can identify a toothbrush and toothpaste, he will not engage in the desired behavior of brushing his teeth. While Johnny will not consistently comply with parent requests, he takes interest in his older sister, Jane, and will often imitate what she does.

In the bathroom that Johnny uses, record a video of Jane completing all steps of the tooth brushing sequence. Record Jane as she puts toothpaste on the toothbrush, places the toothbrush in her mouth, brushes the left side, the right side, and her front teeth, rinses the toothbrush, rinses her mouth, and spits. We will want individual videos of each step, but if it is available to us we can use a video editing program to do this later.

Place a toothbrush and toothpaste identical to the ones used by Jane in the same place she retrieves them from in the video. Load the videos on a cell phone or tablet so that they are easily accessible and set them to loop continuously when played. Bring Johnny to the bathroom and say, "Brush your teeth." Play the first video. Do not initially prompt Johnny at all, simply let the video play. If Johnny does not attend to the video, non-verbally direct him to do so by pointing to it or physically directing his gaze towards it if necessary. If after three to five loops of the video Johnny does not attempt to imitate it, non-verbally and physically prompt him to perform the skill exactly as Jane does in the video. Play the next video and repeat the process. Once all steps are completed, reinforce with praise and a highly preferred item.

Record the amount of prompting required to attend to the video and to complete each step of the skill. Repeat this process once or twice a day (morning and night) until five sessions' worth of data is gathered, and review the data. If the amount of required prompting is decreasing, continue and review again after five sessions. If there are no signs of improvement, it is time to troubleshoot. Is the program being implemented consistently? Is sufficient time being given to view the video? Is Johnny attending to the video? Is the reinforcing item providing enough motivation?

Once the data shows the skill being completed independently and consistently, we can consider fading the video. If we notice Johnny is performing the skill and is no longer watching the video, switch to the original video showing the full task and play this instead, keeping it available for Johnny to refer to if he gets lost. If Johnny continues to perform the task independently without referring to the video, it can be removed entirely, but in the future if Johnny has trouble with the task or asks to see the video, it can be brought back.

7. Building Independence

The ability to perform tasks independently significantly impacts both learner success as well as quality of life. Video modeling can be used to aid in this process by removing a potential barrier to independence, namely our own presence as the teacher!

Typically, we will teach or provide guidance using prompting: the use of a word, command, or action that helps a learner to perform the behavior being targeted. This typically takes one of the following forms:

- *Verbal:* The prompter provides a verbal model of a desired response. This may also come in the form of overemphasizing the correct choice in a situation involving multiple choices, or a cue of the beginning of the response. It is critical that verbal prompts only be utilized when a verbal response is desired.

- *Physical:* The prompter places their hand over the learner's and guides them to perform the targeted behavior.

- *Gestural:* The prompter points to the correct response.

- *Positional:* The prompter physically manipulates the learner into a position that enables the learner to practice a skill.

- *Locational:* The prompter places the correct response in closer proximity to the learner than other choices or possible responses.

- *Modeling:* The prompter performs the targeted behavior so that the learner can replicate it.

Good teaching utilizes prompting techniques and strategies effectively and will fade the prompt as the learner makes progress; for example, the use of a physical prompt will be faded to a gestural prompt, and so forth. However, a potential problem that can occur is that the learner begins to look for, anticipate, or otherwise wait for a prompt before performing a behavior or advancing in a series of steps of a behavior. A common strategy to help with this is to provide prompting from behind the learner whenever possible, removing the prompter from view and making the prompt easier to fade. However, this may not work in all cases, and in some situations the learner may even turn to face the prompter in seeking out the prompt.

I was working with an older learner on the daily living skill of washing windows, but I found that no matter how I presented my prompts, between each step he would look to me again. He would go to the window, and turn to me. He would spray the window, and turn to me. He would wipe the window, and turn to me. A possible solution to a situation like this would be to incorporate visual cues or a visual schedule, but even this may still require some prompting to follow the schedule, such as pointing at the next step. What do we do when it becomes difficult to fade out the prompts to follow the schedule?

The use of a video model moves the source of the prompt away from a person and onto an object, giving the learner less of a motivation to seek out the adult. In the event that the learner's attention wavers or they otherwise go off-task, they should be non-verbally redirected first and foremost back to the video. If the learner is attending properly to the video but requires additional support to perform the behavior, it should be in the form of a non-verbal prompt while remaining out of the learner's field of vision as much as possible.

In the example scenarios that will be discussed in future chapters, the building of independence is secondary to the primary goal being targeted using the video model. Once a learner can perform the behavior demonstrated in a video, begin to fade the video out. The most efficient way of fading video models out is by using chaining.

Chaining is a teaching strategy that involves breaking down a complex skill into its component parts and teaching each step in the chain until the learner can perform the entire task. In a forward chain, the learner is expected to independently perform the task up until the current step. Upon performing the current step, the learner is reinforced and the rest of the chain is prompted. In a backwards chain, the steps of the task are prompted up until the current step, at which point the learner is expected to perform the rest of the task independently and is reinforced. Backwards chaining is typically used in situations where the skill may not make sense to the learner when started from the first step. For example, the act of putting on underwear may be too far away from the act of fully getting dressed that it is not meaningful, and so it is more impactful to begin with the final step; in this case, pulling up the pants once all other clothing items are already on (Ball 2008).

Which method to use will be determined by the learner. If the learner can initiate an activity but not complete it, use forward chaining. If they cannot initially engage but will participate once the activity is underway, use backward chaining. Always remember to systematically fade based on the proficiency of the child, not by the length of time they watched the video. For example, if you were to use a backward chain to teach a play skill, the child would participate in an activity for a period time with the video being turned off for the end of the activity. If the child continues to engage in the activity successfully, the following session the video would be turned off at an earlier point, with future sessions having an earlier and earlier shut off point contingent on the child continuing to perform the skill successfully.

8. Transitions

Individuals with ASD often have difficulty transitioning to new activities, new routines, or changes in general. When we target transitioning as a skill, our goals are to reduce the time for the transition to take place and increase appropriate behavior during transitions, as well as to increase independence and reduce adult prompting and interactions. A basic yet effective way to assist in transitioning an individual with ASD is the use of picture sequences.

These picture sequences may take the form of a visual schedule, which allows an individual to see a picture of an upcoming activity and increase their understanding of the sequence of activities that is to follow. This could be in the form of actual pictures, Meyer-Johnson symbols, objects, or even the written words themselves. When the individual is able to predict the events that will be forthcoming, their own behavior then becomes more predictable and easier to shape to the desired behavior. There have been numerous studies conducted that visual schedules, when implemented in either the classroom or home setting, can assist in decreasing transition time and increasing appropriate behavior, as well as increase student independence (Dettmer et al. 2000).

Just as with picture sequences, videos can be used to show the individual with ASD where they will be going and what they might be doing, thereby showing the individual what the expectations are for what is going to be happening next in their daily life. These videos can take many forms.

One way of doing this is to create a video that will show a first-person perspective, or be from the "mind's eye" of the individual. This allows for the individual watching the video to see exactly what they can expect to see when they perform the activity. For a transition to a new environment, point the video straight ahead and go to the next location, showing each turn and door gone through. This video may be shown to the individual prior to the transition, perhaps even multiple times if necessary. The individual can also take the video along with them to follow its path. This can later be faded to just showing the video, and then to simply a picture of the actual environment.

Ethan was a young man who, once in school, would refuse to leave the room until it was time to go home. Anytime that the staff would attempt to transition him, he would consistently melt down when he came to the same door opening. The issue was that at this particular threshold, turning left meant that Ethan was going home; however, the necessary transitions required going right. Ethan believed each time that they left the room that he was going home, and when he was not allowed to turn left (and go home) he became upset. Pictures and transition objects were used without success. A "mind's eye" video was created and walked the path to the

gymnasium. Once the video arrived at the threshold, it looked left and then right before making the right turn. Ethan was shown the video several times prior to leaving the classroom. The first time he left the room after watching the video, he took it with him. When he got to the threshold, he followed the video: first looking left, and then right. He made the right hand turn and followed it to the gymnasium. The video was able to be faded out after three weeks, and the same technique worked to transition the student to various areas such as the art room, music room, and cafeteria.

Another method would be to take a video of the environment, or simply the person that the individual will be going to see. In the case of a person being visited—perhaps a teacher, therapist, doctor, or family member—the video could include the person talking about what will happen once they arrive. This can also be shown prior to the transition, once or several times as necessary, or taken along if needed. This again can be faded back to simply showing the video prior to transition, or to only a picture.

David was an elementary-aged student who had difficulty transitioning to Speech and Language Therapy. When the therapist would come to escort the student to therapy, David would go without incident. However, when directed to go by himself, he would have a meltdown. With his future in middle school and the anticipated need for greater independence in mind, he needed to learn to navigate the school environment on his own. The staff began by putting a picture of the Speech Language therapist in his individual picture schedule, however, this was not effective and he would still have a meltdown upon leaving the room. Then, a video model was used including the Speech and Language therapist in the therapy room. He was shown the video prior to going, along with a five-minute warning ahead of the transition. The first three times he brought the video with him as he walked; then it was able to be faded to just being viewed prior to leaving, and then back to the original strategy of simply putting the picture of the therapist in the schedule.

Ongoing activities that involve ritualistic or repetitive routines lend themselves well to video modeling. Physical education classes are a great example of this. Class typically follows a routine of an opening exercise set consisting of stretches or simple exercises such as sit-ups or push-ups. The sequence of exercises can be recorded and shown to a student in the classroom prior to the transition to the gym.

Suzy had no problem with traveling to gym class, however, once there would ignore the class and run around the gymnasium. The teacher would begin each class with the same sequence of stretches, exercises, and motor imitation activities. A video was recorded of the teacher standing in the gym, providing instruction and modeling the exercise routine in the same order that is followed in class. Suzy was shown the video in her classroom and prompted to follow and imitate the routine. After several days of success, the video was brought to the gym class, and the video played for Suzy as the teacher led the class parallel to what was happening in the video. With Suzy now complying with the routine alongside her classmates, the video was faded out over the next several class periods, with less and less of the video being shown each period until Suzy was following the teacher directly.

Video modeling can also be used for any special or one-time events, believe it or not. This may include events such as a pep rally or a Halloween parade, or any event that is out of the ordinary for the student. Simply run an internet search for videos of these types of events, or better yet, use video of past events at the school if they exist and are available. Show the student the video several times during the days or hours leading up to the event, allowing them to grow comfortable with the events they are viewing.

Jason was an elementary school student who was very particular about his routine. A week ahead of the school's annual Halloween parade, his teacher was concerned that he would have difficulty participating in what would be a unique event. An internet search for "elementary Halloween parade" brought up many videos of similar school events. Jason was shown these videos in the days leading up to the event, after which his teacher would remind the class of their own parade that was coming up. The day of the event he was shown the video prior to getting changed into his costume and again immediately before going to the parade, and happily participated in the event without incident.

Transition to a community outing, such as a supermarket or retail store, can also be aided by the use of a video model. Expectations for the outing can be very clear and include what is being bought, what is being earned for appropriate behavior, and what exactly is going to happen during the outing. This can also be carried over to visits to friends and family members in the same way.

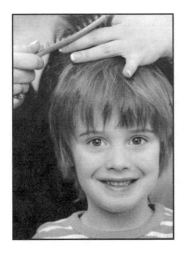

A common question that parents have is about how to prepare their child for a haircut. In a situation like this, it isn't necessary to recreate the wheel. Go online and run a search for kids getting haircuts, and select a video of a child getting a haircut that appears happy about it. Make sure to screen the entire video before showing it to the child, as not every video that starts happy ends happy!

This process can also be successful with car or bus rides by taking a video of the way to go to another school or a field trip. It can be effective when transitioning students from elementary school to middle school, or from middle school to high school, as well. Start by showing pictures of places such as the entrance, the cafeteria, or the gymnasium. Then, introduce a social narrative describing the differences between each transition location. Continue the transition with videos of the new environment or areas of the building, focusing on areas that the student can reasonably expect to access when he or she comes to school, such as offices, the cafeteria, the gym, the library, or the art room. It is best to minimize videos of people or specific classroom locations, as these may change from year to year. Instead, focus on specific areas that are more certain not to change, such as the entrance to the building, the cafeteria, or the gymnasium. While this can have great success in initial transitions, it does not take the place of actual visits and the individual becoming more comfortable with the new environment. This can also be successful with temporary transitions, for example, when a program such as summer school or an extended school year will be held in a different building or area of the current building.

Lights, Camera, Action!

Patty will be beginning a new physical therapy session two nights a week at a private clinic. She often has difficulty transitioning to new environments. Additionally, while she is typically okay with going for a ride in the car, she frequently becomes upset at the destination if it is not a restaurant or otherwise a food establishment.

Record a video using the "mind's eye" perspective of the car ride itself. This is done without Patty being present and should be recorded from her

typical seat in the car, so that the viewpoint presented in the video is as close as possible to the view that Patty herself will see while she is riding. Then record a "mind's eye" video walking from the car into the clinic itself.

Consideration needs to be given to what will be an effective and logistically available reinforcer for success. Given that the endpoint is away from the home, and further demands will immediately be placed upon Patty, typically available reinforcers may be unavailable or impractical. As we know that Patty enjoys eating out, it might work best to add that as a second destination after the session at the clinic is completed.

Both videos should be shown multiple times to Patty prior to the drive, and she can be allowed to watch it during the actual ride, as well. Upon arriving at the clinic, show Patty the video of entering the clinic and allow her to take the video with her for the walk. Upon entering the clinic, reinforce with praise.

If Patty continues to have difficulty with the transition, begin to troubleshoot. Is sufficient time being given to view the video? Does the route being driven match the route shown on the video? Is an effective reinforcer in place? Do you need to make a video of her in the setting during therapy?

If the reinforcer is not being provided until after the therapy session, consider whether this is concrete enough on its own, or if further support is needed. Videos of participation in the session can be added, followed by a video transitioning to the reinforcer. The video of the session may need to be of a model as opposed to the "mind's eye" perspective that has been being used.

Once the transition is being made successfully and consistently, we can consider fading the video. Patty may only need to watch the video prior to leaving. The video may be faded back to just a picture in a schedule. If difficulty resurfaces, the video can always be reinstated as necessary.

9. Play Skills

Studies have shown that video modeling was an effective and efficient strategy for teaching sequences of cooperative play, and these interactive play skills were achieved with relatively short exposure to training and in the absence of response prompting and reinforcement (MacDonald

et al. 2009). Additionally, it has been demonstrated that with an appropriate parent training program in place, parents can be successful when conducting a video modeling intervention with their children in the home (Besler and Kurt 2016).

The key to this type of video modeling is to have individuals with excellent play skills already in place serve as the models in the videos. Once parental permission is acquired, select toys that are in the environment that the child is exposed to everyday, and toys the child will be exposed to in any inclusionary experience. A video of the child with good play skills is then taken. Take about a five-minute video of the child paying with the toy, with all the verbal language typically associated with the play activity. It is critical that the toys in the video are actual toys that the child will encounter in their natural environment. Put the video on a loop and set up a "play center" time with the video running. Prompt the individual to stay in the area where the video is playing, and keep the child in the general area in which the video is playing. Through repetition, the child will begin to pick up the toys and play. Make sure initially that the individual receives a lot of reinforcement for small accomplishments, such as watching the video at first, then picking up the toy, then playing with the toy, and so on. This can be faded into an activity with neuro-typical peers by transferring the video to that environment and then fading it out. The video in the neurotypical environment is also a magnet to get the other students to interact with the child.

A preschool teacher was feeling overwhelmed by the volume of demands she had in terms of what to accomplish with her students. Working with limited time in which she had to address toilet-training and necessary pre-academic skills, there simply wasn't opportunity to work on play skills, and without these skills her students were having trouble interacting with neuro-typical peers in play settings. A neuro-typical peer who had shown appropriate play skills in the integrated setting was recorded playing with toys that were accessible in his classroom, and this video was played on a loop on a smartboard in the classroom in which the same toys were available. Tape was placed on the floor enclosing an area within view of the screen, and staff were given the simple direction to keep students within the marked area. After three weeks of exposure and in the absence of prompting, a non-verbal student imitated a behavior from the video of playing with a truck, and imitated the sound "vroom vroom" that the child in the video made. During this student's natural inclusion time, where he had struggled in the past during play time, the video was brought along and played, and he continued to play appropriately with the truck. With this student now exhibiting appropriate play, other neuro-typical peers began to come over and engage with him. The use of the video also encouraged the other neuro-typical students to come over to see what was going on, allowing more opportunities for interaction.

Lights, Camera, Action!

Leslie is a four-year-old that will not play at home and the only activities she wants to engage in are scripting, lining up toys, and repetitive completion of the same puzzles. The parents are concerned that she is not playing appropriately. She

has an older sibling that tries to play with her, but is unable to because her younger sister will only do what she wants to do and will not engage with other activities.

VIDEO MODELING

Create a video model of the older sister engaging in and playing with other activities that are age-appropriate, such as playing with dolls, a variety of puzzles, coloring, modeling clay, and so forth. Allow Leslie to view the video several times, and then have the video present and looping while the sibling is engaging in the activities. During this time, engage in active teaching, showing the sibling how to appropriately interact with younger sister in a positive manner by doing facilitated play activities such as group games, turn-taking, and other interactive activities.

Once the siblings have begun to interact appropriately, begin fading out the video.

10. Social Skills

The underdevelopment of social skills is a typical aspect of individuals with autism. This often leads to children having difficulty interacting with other children, being unable to play together or understand the rules of group games, and joining with others in general. This lack of social relationships at a young age can lead to decreased access later on to employment or independent living (Strain and Schwartz 2001).

Video modeling procedures have been shown to enhance social initiation of children, and these behavior changes have generalized across peers and settings (Nikopoulous and Keenan 2006). Video modeling has also been shown to be effective in increasing social language (Alcantara 2006), thus giving learners access to integrated settings. As their initiation and language improves, they will have more opportunities to be included with their neuro-typical peers.

A lot of videos of appropriate social behavior already exist and can be found with a simple web search. Many children's programs are built around scenes modeling appropriate social interactions. For school-aged students, appropriate current TV programs can be utilized. For older learners, internet outlets can be used. Always keep in mind to preview all videos before their use. There are occasions when the author of the video will imbed inappropriate content somewhere in the video. There are also pre-packaged commercial videos for purchase. The best way to do social skills video modeling is to video record the learner performing the social skill correctly; then, having fun with it, have them perform the social skill incorrectly. They can be compared and contrasted to help the learner to see what they might look like to others when they perform the social skill incorrectly.

Peer-mediated instruction is one of the most successful evidenced-based strategies, and can be easily incorporated into teaching social skills via video modeling. The use of neuro-typical peers during the initial teaching can lead to better generalization. The neuro-typical peers understand the skills being taught and motivated, and can help to prompt the learner when there are no staff around. Group lessons are the best way to achieve this. Having learners on the spectrum and their neuro-typical counterparts participate together in the lesson will enhance the skills' use down the road. It is important to use multiple peer-mediators so that our learners do not fixate or obsess on a specific peer.

Lucy was an elementary-aged student who presented as significantly challenged, was non-verbal, and typically communicated using an augmentative device. Several staff members felt that she could not be successful in an inclusionary setting due to her challenges. She was placed in a "pod" (a group of four students) in the inclusion classroom based on her ability to be successful with the academic curriculum. The general education teacher and the special education teacher, using a structured social skills curriculum, prioritized the skills they felt were most important for her to be successful in the general education environment, and selected "asking for help" as the first skill to target. The special education teacher pulled the student and her three pod-mates, and prepared a video model of Lucy and the other three students performing the skill both correctly and incorrectly. Afterward, the group compared and contrasted each video. As Lucy was non-verbal, she was also shown to tap on a person's shoulder, as this required more social interaction than simply pushing a button on her device. The group returned to the inclusion classroom with the video model of appropriate behavior available. If the teacher or her pod-mates suspected that Lucy needed help and was not asking for it, they would turn on the video, and she would make the request. A point-reward system was used and Lucy received points for making requests. This allowed for the video to be faded out, and she was successful throughout the year. One of the wonderful things about this interaction is that there was peer-support in addition to teacher-support, and this helped Lucy to generalize the skill to other settings such as the gymnasium or cafeteria.

A lot of established social skills curriculums already utilize visuals as part of the programming. In these situations, it is a simple task to integrate the use of a video model in the program in place of, or as a supplement to, the visuals that are already in place.

Lights, Camera, Action!

Adam is a high school student whose neuro-typical younger brother, Jacob, will be moving up to the high school in September. Adam has been aggressive at home towards his brother in the past and has a history of becoming upset when items or people, particularly his brother, appear in places where they do not belong. Their parents are concerned that Adam will have trou-

ble adjusting to seeing his brother during the school day. While they would never be in class together, it is possible that they would cross paths in the hallway or encounter each other in the cafeteria during lunch time. Their parents want for Adam to interact appropriately with Jacob during these instances.

Bring Adam to the cafeteria and record a video of him hav-

ing an appropriate social interaction with his teacher, but be sure that only Adam appears in the actual video. Separately, have Jacob come to the high school and record him in the cafeteria performing the appropriate responses to what Adam does in his video, again making sure that only Jacob appears in the video. Edit the two videos together to produce a video that appears to show Adam and Jacob interacting with each other in the cafeteria.

Allow Adam to watch the video several times until he is comfortable with it, both in the classroom and in the cafeteria. Once September arrives, be sure that Adam has the video with him in the cafeteria and play it any time Jacob is present. This should be done in conjunction with facilitated social activities to teach Adam appropriate ways to interact with his brother.

11. Teaching Skills

Video modeling often facilitates rapid skill acquisition, maintenance, and generalization across settings, people, and materials (Delano 2007), all of which are key aspects to learning. "Skill acquisition" is how a student learns new knowledge as the result of instruction or exposure. "Maintenance" is the act of repeating or rehearsing a skill so that it does not weaken or fade. "Generalization" is when a learner can perform a behavior in different settings or places, with different people, and with various materials; for example, being able to say hello to both the classroom teacher as well as the cashier in the cafeteria and the secretary in the principal's office, or being able to make a simulated purchase in the classroom as well as for real at a fast food restaurant. The key component to making all of these aspects successful, especially for learners with autism, is consistency and predictability. This decreases anxiety and allows students to have an awareness of what is coming next, putting them in a better position to learn. The bottom line is always about the learning process.

Chris was a middle school student who was having over one hundred aggressions a day. After an assessment, it was hypothesized that the aggression was maintained by escape from demands. His teacher used all the typical strategies to address escape-maintained behaviors, such as a motivation system, use of a break card, and so forth. It was decided to attempt video modeling so instructions would be given consistency. A video model was created for each of his programs. An independent schedule was created, and as Chris followed his schedule and moved to each activity, the instruction would come from the video model. The quantity of aggressions decreased from over one hundred to a minimal level in the span of only a few days. After a couple months, the video began to be faded using a backwards chain, with the teacher providing direct instruction for the final activity of the day. Ultimately, it appeared as though a behavior that was motivated by escape was really a product of inconsistency and unpredictability, and the use of a video model was the solution.

If a student is able to handle the rigor of a general education classroom, but has problem behavior or other challenges that prevent the student from being able to be physically present in the setting, this could be addressed through the use of video. The student could be set up with an individual study carrel and video chat into the general education class, or in the case of behavior that was disruptive enough to interrupt the learning process, recorded video of the teaching leading the gen-ed classroom can be played in the individual setting. Most school settings have this capacity and do not even realize it. If the classroom is equipped with Smart Technology, there is a built-in video capacity already available. Also, if the gen-ed teacher uses a certain type of projector, this can also be shown via video chat programs. When all else fails, you can always default to the use of a tablet.

A middle school student previously had a successful academic career, but this had been in an elementary school in which he was in the same classroom with the same teacher all day. After transitioning to middle school, he was now in an environment where his classroom and teacher would change throughout the day. He would enter a classroom and have a melt-down that, for him, consisted of pulling his hoodie over his head and putting his head down on his desk. After the first semester, he was failing all of his classes, and it was determined that it was not the product of the work being too difficult. He was set up in a special education classroom in his own study carrel and used an online video chat with his academic classes, but still participated in specials (art, music, gym) and lunch in the cafeteria for socialization purposes. The special education teacher would gather all of his work from the other teachers each day so that all materials were available in the carrel.

About six months into the school year he was moved back into the general education setting, beginning with the classes in which he was having more success and seemed to enjoy. By the end of the year, he was fully included back in all classes. The following year, anticipating a similar process, he began in the special education classroom with the video chat in place—with the exception of his most preferred subject, math. Meanwhile, video models were used in advance to show him what all of his upcoming teachers would look and sound like. The second year, he had been transitioned into all of his classes by a few months into the school year. By his last year in middle school, he was given the choice of starting the year with the video chat method or going directly into the classrooms on day one. By this point, he had made the adjustment and chose to go to each of his classes.

Similar strategies can be used to address other circumstances in which anxiety affects performance. For example, in the case of a selective mute student who can communicate and interact in specific situations outside of school, but will not speak in school or in the presence of particular people (such as a teacher). Have someone come to school with whom the child will speak, and record a video of an interaction in which only the child can be seen. It will likely be necessary to set up the video on a tripod or have the parent record the video, as the presence of a third person to operate the video may cause the child to not speak. Record a second video of the teacher in the same setting saying everything that the parent said in the first video, and then edit the two videos together so that it appears the student and teacher are having a conversation directly. Have the student watch the edited video while praising the simulated interaction, and this will allow the student to become more comfortable with the idea and decrease the anxiety that it causes.

Video modeling can also be highly effective in teaching domestic and personal care skills. We often teach these skills using picture sequences, but additional prompting is often required and can be difficult to fade. Tooth-brushing is a great example of a skill that can be taught using a picture sequence, but those sequences may not be enough as specific movements are a key part of the behavior chain. A video model will demonstrate the motions needed to complete the skill, without the need for an adult to model or prompt the motion. This visual support can always be available and used where ever the learner is.

"Shaping" is the concept of reinforcing approximations of behavior, over time moving the acceptable approximation closer to the target behavior, and this strategy can be supported through the use of video modeling. For example, a child uses an idiosyncratic motion—such as shaking their hand—to request the bathroom, when the American Sign Language motion is to place the thumb between the index and middle finger while making a fist and quickly moving the wrist back and forth. Initially, you would praise the idiosyncratic motion, while physically prompting the correct response and granting the request. Then, gradually change the acceptable approximation—such as moving the wrist while making a fist—until the request is being made correctly. To support this with video modeling, record a video of each successive acceptable approximation, and show the learner the next incremental approximation to use as a model when it is time to make the request. This makes it a very consistent way to teach the skill.

Lights, Camera, Action!

Bryan is learning to do laundry, a daily living skill. A task analysis has been completed for the skill to break it down into a chain of smaller skills, such as loading and unloading the machines, moving the laundry from one machine to the other, adding necessary liquids, and folding the laundry.

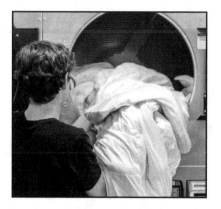

Even with the skill broken down into steps and with appropriate prompting strategies being utilized for a forward chaining procedure, Bryan is struggling with the skill. A visual schedule was put in place, but he still requires a significant amount of prompting.

Record a video model of each of the steps of the task analysis so that there is one video that shows the entire procedure of doing the laundry. Allow Bryan to view the video in its entirety several times before attempting to perform the skill. When it comes time to actually do the task, have the video play and loop it so Bryan sees the entire procedure over and over again.

12. Vocational Skills

Take a moment and think about how you received training in the jobs that you have worked during your lifetime. In most jobs, it was likely at least one of three ways: a video training module, a picture sequence of required tasks, or being paired with a staff member that can model the job for the first day or two. Yet in many programs, the current model of Community Based Instruction (CBI) that is used for vocational training is for a job coach to accompany a student one-on-one and prompt the completion of assigned tasks. However, a reliance on the job coach can emerge, and this structure does not generalize well to adult services programs, which often have staffing ratios of one staff person to every ten to fifteen clients, or more.

The use of a video model in this situation creates the opportunity for increased independence and lessened need for staff, in addition to teaching an easily generalized skill of following the video model. This significantly lessens the challenge of making the transition to adult services.

I was in charge of a vocational lab for high school students in which the goal was to replicate the work environment as much as possible. We had designed a series of "mind's eye" videos showing how to complete the tasks, and used an app to make it so that the videos would loop and continue to play. Adam was a young man who we felt didn't need the video modeling support due to our perceptions of his skill level and independence. One day, his assigned task involved wrapping plastic hamburgers in a simulation of food preparation in a fast food restaurant or cafeteria. As I circulated the room, I noticed the quality of his wrapping was sub-standard and would be unappealing to a consumer. Rather than draw his attention to it, I retrieved a tablet and loaded the video model; I simply walked past his station and placed the tablet on his desk with the video running, without so much as a word or otherwise acknowledging anything, and continued to circulate the room. The video showed a "mind's eye" perspective of two hands laying out the burger and paper, and slowly went through the steps of folding the paper and wrapping the burger. After a few moments I heard a quiet "oh." The next time I passed his station, I noticed that all of the mistakes had been corrected to a perfect quality. At the conclusion of the session, I praised Adam for his good work, and he thanked me for giving him the video as a guide.

This can easily be transferred to on-site job experiences. Record a video of anticipated tasks being completed at the job site. Replicate the task in the classroom and have the student complete the task using the video as a guide. When the student is able to complete the task and is ready to begin at the job site, bring the video and allow the student to continue to view the video while completing the task.

Jake was scheduled to begin a job-sampling term working at a local thrift store. His assigned task would be working in the back area of the store, taking clothing that had been donated and hanging it on a rack. Ahead of Jake beginning work, a video was taken on the job-site of his

teacher completing the task, exactly as Jake would later be expected to do it. The task was simulated in his classroom, and Jake watched the video of his teacher on the job-site prior to completing the simulated activity. This was done several times in the week prior to beginning work. On his first day of work, Jake was shown the video during the ride to the store, and again prior to beginning the task. He completed the task correctly and made a successful transition to the job-site.

A skill related to vocational environments that can be overlooked is taking a break appropriately. It is not uncommon for our learners to be uncomfortable or unaware of what to do in these situations. This can be addressed through the use of a video model demonstrating appropriate potential behaviors, or perhaps a social story in video form that shows the process of taking a break—such as listening to music with headphones in a break room, getting coffee or water, or having an appropriate social interaction with a coworker as described previously in the Social Skills chapter.

VIDEO MODELING

Jay was participating in a structured learning experience in which he was working in an office setting filing paperwork. While he could successfully complete the task, Jay was often unwilling to take breaks or step away from incomplete work. The job coach hypothesized that this was, in large part, due to Jay not understanding or accepting that he would be able to return to the task at the end of the break, and was unwilling to transition away from an incomplete task. A video model was utilized showing the sequences of steps: leaving the work at the station, purchasing a snack from the vending machine, sitting in the break room and eating the snack, and returning to the work station to resume work. Jay watched the video several times and was able to follow the steps, and it was not long before he accepted the routine and was able to take breaks on his own, understanding that he would be able to complete his work afterwards.

Lights, Camera, Action!

Shawn is scheduled to begin working at a warehouse where his primary assignment will be to build boxes that will later be used to ship product. While his parent-and-child study team all agree that he is ready for this placement, it will be a new task in a new location, and he has had some trouble in similar situations in the past.

Begin by going to the worksite and record a video of the task being performed in the environment, manner, and procedure that Shawn will later be expected to complete. This may be either a "mind's eye" or third-person video, dependent upon what will best benefit Shawn.

To the extent in which it is possible, recreate the environment of the worksite and the anticipated task in the classroom. This should include using the actual materials, in this case the boxes, that are utilized in the warehouse. Have the materials presented the same way that they will be presented in the warehouse, be it on a shelf, lying on a table, or however the case may be.

Allow Shawn to view the video and then perform the task in the classroom just as it will later be performed at the worksite. If the task will be performed while standing at the worksite, it should be performed while standing in the classroom. Even if the task is being performed independently, do not fade the video yet as one of the goals at this point is to pair the video with the task so it will generalize to the worksite.

When Shawn is ready to begin his job placement, he should bring the video with him and view it during the ride to the site, and again at the worksite prior to beginning work. Allow the video to play while Shawn is completing the task. Once he is comfortable and successful in the task, the video can begin to be faded.

If there are concerns or challenges related to the transition to the worksite, we may want to use a video as discussed previously in the Transitions chapter.

13. Final Scene!

You're nearly ready! When considering the use of video modeling, keep in mind the key benefits of the predictability and ease of use.

For many learners with autism, a significant struggle and barrier to success is the anxiety that they have as a result of not knowing what is about to happen or what comes next. A video model, particularly a looping one, is predictable. The student has seen the video previously, it is familiar, and it will become memorable. With the anxiety produced by unpredictability now eliminated or lessened, the student becomes available for learning.

With considerations of modern technology, video modeling is extremely accessible, which makes it easy to use by family members and professional staff. A video model can be produced quickly on a cell phone, and the availability of cell phones allows for the immediate availability of a video model for support.

Remember the process of utilizing a video model:

- Exposure: Allowing the video model to play in the presence of the learner without prompting, so that they can become comfortable with it at their own pace.

- Repetition: The repeated viewing of the video so that the learner familiarizes themselves with it.

- Familiarity: The point of being comfortable with the video so that it is now predictable.

- Engagement: The point the learner is now actively involved and interested in the video.
- Risk-Taking: Having learned a new skill, another door is opened for greater success.
- Integration: Making the skill work in real life.

Our learners typically require external motivation to advance and make progress: either in the form of tangible reinforcement and praise, or provided by a system of reinforcement that is individualized to the learner. Video models are no different, and the learner will benefit from their reinforcement system being utilized to support the use of the video. Learners should be reinforced for following the model and completing the targeted behaviors, with stronger and more powerful reinforcement being used for the successful and independent completion of tasks.

The use of video modeling should be incorporated into the development of a learner's Individualized Education Plan (IEP). While the most obvious way to do this is by including it as a support in the accommodations and strategies section of an IEP, we can also develop goals and objectives related to the use of video modeling. These goals should be specific, measurable, and observable.

Some examples of appropriate goals and objectives incorporating video modeling are as follows:

- Given a video model, Adam will independently greet his peers 80 percent of the time.
- Given a video model, Bryan will independently fold the laundry in three consecutive sessions.
- Given a video model, Leslie will independently take her turn while playing a group game in four out of five opportunities.
- Given a video model, Shawn will independently complete his assigned task at a job site with 90 percent accuracy.

Now you're ready to arm your students with lifelong skills that will enable them to become more independent and improve their quality of life, while increasing their dignity and self-worth!

And remember ... lights ... camera ... action!

References

Alcantara. 2006. "Effects of Video Modeling and Video Feeback on Peer-Directed Social Language Skills of a Child with Autism." *Journal of Positive Behavior Interventions.* 8 (2): 106-118.

Ball, J. 2008. Early Intervention & Autism: *Real-Life Questions, Real-Life Answers.* Arlington: Future Horizons.

Besler, F., and Kurt, O. 2016. "Effectiveness of Video Modeling Provided by Mothers in Teaching Play Skills to Children with Autism." *Educational Sciences: Theory & Practice.* 16(1): 209-230.

Chan, J.M., Lang, R., Rispoli, M., O'Reilly, M., Sigafoos, J., and Cole, H. 2009. "Use of peer-mediated interventions in the treatment of autism spectrum disorders: A systematic review." *Research in Autism Spectrum Disorders*, 3: 876-889.

Charlop, M, and Milstein, J. 1989. "Teaching Autistic Children Conversational Speech Using Video Modeling." *Journal of Applied Behavioral Analysis.* 22 (3): 275-285.

Delano, M. 2007. "Video Modeling Interventions for Individuals with Autism." *Remedial and Special Education.* 28 (1): 33-42.

Dettmer, S., Simpson, R., Myles, B., and Ganz, J. 2000. "The Use of Visual Supports to Facilitate Transitions of Students with Autism." *Focus on Autism and Other Developmental Disabilities.* 15: 163-169.

MacDonald, R., Sacramone, S., Mansfield, R., Wiltz, K., and Ahearn, W. 2009. "Using Video Modeling to Teach Reciprocal Pretend Play to Children with Autism." *Journal of Applied Behavioral Analysis.* 42 (1): 43-55.

Nikopoulous, K., and Keenan, M. 2006. "Using Video Modeling to Teach Complex Social Sequences to Children with Autism." *Journal of Autism and Developmental Disorders.* 37 (4): 678-693.

Strain, P.S., and Schwartz, I. 2001. "ABA and the Development of Meaningful Social Relations for Young Children with Autism." *Focus of Autism and Other Developmental Disabilities.* 16: 120-128.

About the Author

 Steve Lockwood, a board-certified Behavior Analyst, has been working with learners with autism of all ages for over fifteen years. He is a Special Education teacher, has presented at numerous conferences including the Autism Society National Conference and ABA International Conference, and has been published in *Autism Asperger's Digest* magazine. He also provides consultation to families regarding parent training and home support services.

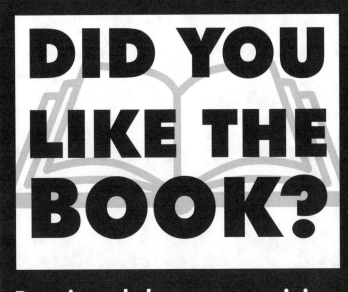